Water in Every Room

Water in Every Room

poems by

Heather Brown Barrett

Cover design by Shay Culligan
Cover image by Kate Aleksandrova
Author photo by Pamela Brown

ISBN: 978-1-63980-707-9

Kelsay Books
502 South 1040 East, A-119
American Fork, Utah 84003
Kelsaybooks.com

for my son

water is life
and with you, we overflow

Acknowledgments

Gratitude is given to the editors of the publications in which the following poems first appeared, some in slightly different versions:

AvantAppal(achia): "Cooking Duck"
BUBBLE Literary Magazine: "Finger Painting"
The Ekphrastic Review: "Baby Boy, Born at 34 Weeks," "House Restored," "How Fierce," "Tending"
Visual Verse: "Blue Moon"
Yellow Arrow Journal: "Growing a Mother"

Contents

Blue Moon

October 31, 2020

Once, in a blue moon, sphere aglow,
desire woke us from our slumber
of lesser onus, an ancient appetite upon us.

Two famished wolves trapped within
our own doors, hungry for more
life, for purpose, for progeny to raise

toward the heavens, and higher,
the bedroom burning, a tidal fire,
engulfed in waves until we drowned

in Yes. We said, Oh come
be our child, wind of change, blow down
this stagnant house, and quick—

midnight pulled you in, raised a blaze
of hope from darkest hour, and later,
as we handed sweets to trick-or-treaters

bundled in costume and coat, you spun
on the backs of our fingers. A secret
only we conceived.

I Touch a Dead Cat the Day My Water Breaks

Danger, an impending rush of cars, looms around the sharp curve of road near my driveway—the reason a cat lies dead in the verdure, halting my walk. Wind gusts and a dried leaf bounces down the asphalt so fast it sounds like a rattlesnake. I crouch and crab-crawl deep into the ditch flush with morning dew and croaking frogs. One hand cradles my thirty-week belly, the other strokes cold black fur. No grey speckles the coat. It's not my beloved cat, but a stray, or a neighbor's. A crow screams and leaves the white blooms of a dogwood tree. The crickets weep, high-pitched, continuous. Vultures will gather later in the heat of the sun and their fetid lure, and blowflies will impregnate a shredded carcass.

      dusk quickens
      amniotic waterfall
      baby   still   moves

Baby Boy, Born at 34 Weeks

Your bloom is so great

and so small,
only four pounds

and seven ounces; my heart,
you burst

from my body, a blossom

still perfect. Every life
is a flower

plucked from ignorance;
we thrive

and wither through our seasons
in this earthen urn,

beautiful in our arrangement
of certain decay.

My son, flourish

bright and brave, for one day
you, too, will fade.

You are my only
heavenly blue morning

glory in this wilted world.

Tending

The NICU hums a low tone of medical instruments and computer fans. I switch off the phototherapy bulb in my son's incubator. He wears a miniature eye mask, a plastic tube snaked through his nostril to his stomach. Cords link his chest to machine. I unlatch and lift the fiberglass sidewall, scoop my hands underneath his warm body, gather him to my sternum. He stays asleep. I settle my sore pelvis into a wheeled chair in his corner of the ward, remove his eye mask. Bow my head to his hair and inhale.

He smells sweet, intoxicates me
like newly-turned earth, a fresh field
to sow my heart into. His tiny fingers
soft as moss, skin hued amber
from early arrival.

His fingerprints
are a maze, a path, a map
leading back to tended roots,
twisting through shade and sun,
plots of sweet corn, summer
squash, butterbeans and brassica.

The NICU doctors and interns begin their morning circuit, murmur in a cluster under the dimmed fluorescence. *How-to* and *Don't-do* posters advise from the walls. A screen above me squiggles out vitals: oxygen, body temp, pulse. Silent numbers satisfy a nurse, who opens and closes doors, drawers, checks supply stock. Her sneakers squeak down the row of dozing infants. My son wakes, tilts his face upward. I bundle him closer.

His blue eyes, deeper than sky,
open wide, graze the gold-flecked forests
of mine.

We're an olive branch, sweet-
grass, a lemon grove, a meadow
of dandelion, goldenrod, and clover.

We're a newborn continent
unto ourselves.

Postpartum

mother is delivered

to an ache of hours
and muscle,

dwelling like a bruise
in flux, weeping

milk, ticking down
the moons,

until drawn

out of herself

Cooking Duck

Undone,
> I hallucinate when fevered. I'm not ill
> but feverishly cooking this duck,

more raw
> since last check, skewered
> by thermometer, its temperature down,

not done,
> my infant's temperature up,
> husband quarantined and fevered too,
> I'm checking thisstupidduck,

again and again,
> hallucinating as I return to the oven,

over and over,
> the baby skewers my earhole
> with a shriek, the cat weaves
> around my feet, mewing at a fever pitch,

undone,
> every creature in this house hot
> except this awful fowl,

still undone,
> should be roasted by now, it's been hours
> or days or maybe a month. This is
> a comedy roast, joke's on me, looking

undone,
> to double check the stove's on.
> I will not eat this duck
> even when finally, thoroughly

DONE—
> cooked, meat sliding off the bone.
> I'll stick to cooking chicken nuggets
> from now on.

Sustenance

We eat burnt salmon from a hot skillet, stabbing it with forks, too tired to sit or find a plate or clean the splattered grease. Hollow bellies gurgle at the offering. We chat about our lack of sleep and desire for hot showers, how hungry we are. Sunlight casts across the floor and our four-month-old's torso as he lounges in his bouncer, watching the ceiling fan whirl. The cat loops the kitchen, bumps the baby each pass. Our son coughs out a giggle—a new skill! We still, surprised silent. He cough-laughs again, and the sound draws us from gloomy self-pity, clinging like marlin to the lure. We chortle back and forth, every wave his wonder, his joy the feast we surface for. The cat, starved for cuddles but rich in leftovers, leaps up to lunch forgotten on the stovetop.

ocean of life
gliding through, tip of scales
gutted at the thought

Thrown

You had a fitful night of feeding and fuss,
squirm and squeak and half-sleep,
the dark hours crushing

my silent ache
for slumber.

You jabber
into my neck

as the morning sun
throws a tantrum of light
through the gapped window curtain.

Ars Horae

The hours con-

fuse into one epoch, a wave
unbroken since the dawn of child;

persistence their strong hand

as they gather and wilt
on the lawn. My frame drapes
like a carcass, too

exhausted in the continuum

after birth, unable to remember
if I wake or dream or lie

lingering in the brilliant sun.

Growing a Mother

Tender words shook my bones
loose, rattled like seeds
in a coffee tin. Milk, bundle, baby,
mother. I was undeserving to grow
a baby from soiled skin, this body
I vilified. My hands
dug into dirt, burying myself
in a field of shortcomings, real
or groundless, shaking
where I was green. My son dawned
early, vulnerable but hardy;
now he is bamboo, sturdier than I,
he is honeysuckle vine, sweet
in his spring. My shoulders bloom
vibrant colors, I grow
a mother and child, embracing
duality; our roots weave joy
with devotion, my hands tending
his body, healing mine.

Bones of My Bones

Years from now I will write a love note
on a heart-shaped post-it
and bury it under a muffin
in your plastic dinosaur lunch box,
telling you to have a good day

like this day,
as you sit in your highchair
holding a blue stuffed brachiosaurus,
your mouth meeting its neck
in a muffled growl.

I will give you kits
to assemble Jurassic jungles,
with little vertebrae and tubes of glue,

and teach you to build
solid skeletons with the bones
of your imagination,
to dig deeper, through the cartilage
into the marrow,

my voracious son.

How Fierce

They never ask how fierce
I am, armored in feathers, talons
sharpened to points, my vigilance
a whirl of white ice, violent
movement as I break open
the whole sky in a flock

of fury; I am blue bruises
on their peripheral, an afterimage
that leaves them frozen, a stone
in their hands. Angel or bird,
wrath or love? They never ask.
My son, I am your protector
and fierce I am.

Curious Words

Years from now you may say *don't*
write a love note
on a yellow post-it, you're too old
for childish displays, so I'll say
Have a good day

like this day,
as you sit in my lap
watching me sing the ABC's,
your mouth shaping and unshaping
to mimic mine.

I will give you magnets,
a neon alphabet to group and regroup
on the refrigerator door,

and teach you to spell
your intent, to articulate the world.
Choose words wisely,

my inquisitive son.

Finger Painting

My son considers his painted palms in our kitchen, wonderstruck
at this new activity. One hand yellow, the other blue,
his first finger painting on the wide paper in front of him.
Big blue whirls meet sunshine yellow, smears of green

where the colors overlap. An ocean churning. He is not afraid
of water. During baths he dips his face in and comes up
laughing, sometimes sniffs it up his nose, and I tell him
We can't breathe under water. Except we can—we cut our gills

like teeth on daily experience. Eyes wide open, gasping for insight.
Science says we started as fish, gill slits already in place.
I don't know if God has gills, but I do know water
is life. How we move through it, breathing in the depth

of love or newness. A churning ocean in our chests.
My son waves his masterpiece back and forth, opens his mouth
and coughs out a laugh. A vague red line forms on his neck.
I run my thumb over it, tell him it's time for a bath.

Grit

My toddler grates his teeth and people groan,
suck in through their own, ask how I can stand it,

the grit of tooth on tooth. I can't waste seconds
gnashing teeth against barbs, or choking
on words unsaid. How hard this is,

tending two lives; my tongue leaves me
stranded, thrashing in the threat of conversation.
How heavy the weight of words in sand.

Some people say I'm a real woman now,
as if I wasn't real before I clenched my teeth
and pushed myself into them, and still

others say he's worth it all, as if I don't know
my own son is worth his weight in water
in a world of drought. I drink his joy

in swells, my mouth an ark of stone;
thirsty until my hands wake, until they pry
open my own jaw. I offer my son

a glass, his tiny teeth chomping at the bit
of boyhood before him, his little hands
clutching as I tell him to sip slow.

Our teeth begin in utero, ready to cut
through generations of taboo.

The quiet grind, each day, a steady shaping
of my interior. Silence builds

within cerebrum and skull,
skin and rib bone, cavern of breast.
I render and rebuild what tooth is left.

Mother Is the Lamb, the Lion

Flare up like flame
and make big shadows I can move in.
—Rainer Maria Rilke, "Go to the Limits of Your Longing"

mother is the lamb, the lion
stalks, the shape-shifter
traps & consumes
herself, lays the bones
to circle 'round: the lamb
lit afire! who is this

woman, this flare
of will & marrow? limbs
resurrect: lion, lamb,
begins again, devours
to strengthen, her sacrifice
the sacred mother's life

Guilt and Confection

The mother eats chocolate and screams
in her head, as if chocolate is primal
rage to conquer. Alone in the front seat

of her parked car, beneath the grey sky
and bowed pecan tree for cover,
she gnashes confection like it's a sin

to want room for herself in these slow days.
Two minutes—the time to read a poem
or eat a candy bar or seize her breath
from the brink of battle cry.

Her subdued shriek matches her son's
refusal to nap, swallows cocoa
square by square. It's ok to have a bit

of silence or devour her own
guilty heart. Her real heart waits

in a red shirt at the doorway
of their house, and his three-foot frame
jump jump jumps like a pulse,

a signal to bring her back indoors.
He is so much sweeter than her

dark morsel of distress. It's gone—
her chocolate. Her grievance. She smooths
the crumpled wrapper, its creases
tiny constellations on a paper night sky.

The mother licks her fingers clean,
her heart now opening the door.

Come Full Circle

Child we'd said, and you came through
as we stood at the edge of birth and wondered
how you would fit. Twenty-two months later
you know basic shapes and colors and extras
like hexagon and trapezoid and violet.
You point and identify as evening blues us

in the sun's waning amber. *Grey rock,* you say.
Green leaf. Black bug. Grinning, *Bug shape!*
All people have them, you continue. *Red flowers,*
drawn to azaleas that match the cerise sky
as sunset arcs over. You pluck one, *Dead flower,*
because you've watched us deadhead the pansies

and we say that it's not dead
but you say *Yes* and nod once, assuring us
it is now. You carry it back to the quilt
strewn with toys and trinkets and expertly grab
and spin an old plastic sorting sphere,
pushing flower and shapes into shaped holes.

Mama, Daddy. Get in, as if we could
fall into your imagination, that wondrous rabbit hole,
and we do. We already jumped
into the unknown of rearing, unsure of depth
or shaping required, but willing to show no fear
should hold us from a leap of faith

come full circle. Get in, son—existence is shaped
by paradoxical potential and you are a god
with play and pun. *Daddy, Mama,* to make sure
we're watching. You arc a red block
over the sorting sphere and declare
Square shape in circle hole!

Active Imagination

You dump a bucket of building blocks and butt-scoot a path through. Smiling stuffies slump together on the end table, watching from under lamp light. The living room is a sea of debris. Beige carpet awash in colorful toys. Your dad and I fold clean laundry from the mountain on the couch, lay each piece gently in the basket. The mound does not seem to shrink. I imagine it bubbling forth from the couch cushions. A wellspring of clothes and towels. You dart to the basket, hover over it, then pick up and fling, one by one, unleashing pants, socks, dishcloths. Grinning like a happy, careless god. We let chaos unfold before us. The cat eyes all from the apex of her carpeted ivory tower. I mention that it's almost time to clean up. Almost time for bed. You frog-hop to the middle of the room, then rock stiff-legged foot to foot, point at objects and holler *Idea! Idea! Idea! Idea!* A frisson of delight fires through me. Your dad quips *Yep, you get that from your mother.*

silent hours
asleep in a book
bittersweet

When I Dream of Cleaning

I'm in a house getting bigger. Not me,
but the house. Maybe I confuse myself
with a house. But I'm not

in Wonderland. I'm in a messy domicile
and yet I'm not
crying, but harried, a hairsbreadth
from spillover,

a specter
wandering dark halls while disheveled
rooms e x p a n d in time-
lapse, frame by frame. A silent film
of grime weeps down

the mantel mirror,
the furnishings,
the doorways,
the laundry,
the toys,
the tv,
me.

Grunge on the mirror glass
ripples, as if
disturbed by lurkings underneath.

My footing unmoors. Maybe
I'm a house again. But I wasn't
solid at the start.

I am out
of minutes, hours, understanding
nothing in this scene of excess
dirt and delay,
this continuum of chagrin

that breaks

        me.

A heavy squall rends my own
echo—oh!—until I'm flooded. Water
in every room. And in this dream

I do not drown but drink myself
a cup of salted sea.

As I rise,
sunlight shines from every angle,
tears down the sodden walls
and remains.

House Restored

I'm a dwelling of many
rooms, a dollhouse
cut in half, full of skulls.
A house prepared

for a child. You see
me in every square
foot, gripping the ledge;
my past a tome

written on a stone
foundation, sinking
in depths, algae-grown,
quiet and heavy.

I set my guilt
outside, lay grace
like a doormat.
You see, this place

is not shame, but color
and laughter; body
forgiven, built upon,
a house repaired

by love. My son
the key cut from faith.
My temple of bones
now sings.

Monolith

Wayward the wind and water breaking
in a youngin storm—all torrents and spills

and cataracts in the eye. Child is a current
of salt and sough and sinew churning

from sea to sky to land
on marram ledge and back again,

and mother is a lighthouse, beholder,
her spine a concrete monolith

of loam and steel, bone-
bare and beacon in the lightening foam

of cloudbreak. She's furious devotion
to his fury of unknowing,

footed where the shore is still, waiting
for his clearing gaze or quiet sigh of sleep.

But his curious winds rise again
on bittersweet air and wave, to roam

in ebb tide or brackish deep or welkin stretch
alone, and leave her weathered tower

standing on the edge of age
and fading.

Prelivers & 20 Keys

We're going to sea, you say, *in our ship*
    and leap onto the couch, which creaks like an old vessel,
        clad in your new medieval suit of armor.
           Shield and greaves, helmet with chin guard,
               plastic clonk of gauntlets against chestplate.
        A sailor's costume might better suit the seas
    but I don't say so because knights board ships too.
You pretend to buckle me in   *chickuh*
then yourself and two sloths slumped between us.
   chickuh   chickuh chickuh
        Fists grip air as you steer through uncharted ocean.
            Full spleen ahead! Ahoy! you urge.
               Prelivers and 20 keys!   We're pirates
        exacting a toll or searching for Precambrian critters
        without livers or spines or spleens.
    We maneuver through play like octopods.
You sheath a toy sword between cushions,
        remark that we're thirsty   and I know this game,
            hold an imaginary cup as you tilt and pour yours
               into mine and the stitched grins of spineless stuffies.
            shhhhhhhh   Lips rounded, sounding like a faucet.
        We swill in rolling gurgles, full throttle,
        heads tipped back like swashbucklers gorging on grog.
We're drunk on nonsense and bottomless brew.
The waves are thiiiiis big. Wooooosh, you sigh
    then crash like an armored invertebrate
        into my unarmored chest.
           We're going over! you holler   and this is like a dream
             I had when I was pregnant with you
        of a tall, tall ship with narrow windows,
     the sunlight swallowed by a swell
and silent weightlessness subdued my fear of falling.

I am head over heels, full tilt in this epic of ours.
   You point a small finger in quick succession,
      Unbuckle unbuckle un un un.   So free. Show me
         how to surge through high seas
            because water is life   and there is so much of it.

Notes

"Ars Horae" is an ekphrastic poem inspired by *The Persistence of Memory,* Salvador Dali (1931).

"Baby Boy, Born at 34 Weeks" is an ekphrastic poem inspired by *Roses, Convolvulus, Poppies and Other Flowers in an Urn on a Stone Ledge,* Rachel Ruysch (1680s).

"Blue Moon" is an ekphrastic poem inspired by an image by Kitty Harrison and Dylan Sauerwein at *Visual Verse,* Vol. 10, Chapter 11 (contemporary).

"Come Full Circle" is an ekphrastic poem inspired by *A Lonesome Border,* Carmella Dolmer (contemporary). This poem was featured in the Suffolk Center for Cultural Arts *Everyone Has a Story* exhibit, December 14, 2023–February 3, 2024.

"House Restored" is an ekphrastic poem inspired by *The Skt. Wandanna Cathedral in Band Hain,* Adolf Wolfli (1910).

"How Fierce" is an ekphrastic poem inspired by *Song of Love,* Nita Jawary (contemporary).

"Monolith" is an ekphrastic poem inspired by *Lighthouse at the Edge of the World,* G. G. Silverman (contemporary), and Ursula K. Le Guin's poem, "On the Western Shore." This poem received First Place for Poetry at the Hampton Roads Writers 15th Annual Writers' Conference, November 2023, and was featured in the Suffolk Center for Cultural Arts *Everyone Has a Story* exhibit, December 14, 2023–February 3, 2024.

"Tending" is an ekphrastic poem inspired by *Green Terrain,* Kelly Austin-Rolo (contemporary).

About the Author

Heather Brown Barrett is an award-winning poet in southeastern Virginia. She mothers her young son and contemplates life, the universe, and everything with her writer husband. She is a board member of Hampton Roads Writers, a member and regular student of The Muse Writers Center, and a member of The Poetry Society of Virginia.

Her poetry has appeared in *The Ekphrastic Review, Yellow Arrow Journal, Black Bough Poetry, AvantAppal(achia),* and elsewhere. Her work is featured on the Dahlgren Railroad Heritage Trail as part of The Poetry Society of Virginia's Poetry on the Trail project.

www.ingramcontent.com/pod-product-compliance
Lightning Source LLC
Chambersburg PA
CBHW030815090426
42737CB00010B/1289